CONFIDENT
Conversations

EASY ANSWERS TO 38 TOUGH QUESTIONS

BRAD DEHAVEN

CONFIDENT Conversations

Easy Answers to 38 Tough Questions

Brad DeHaven

Editor – Catherine Nanton
Cover Designer – Lori Chollar
Layout & Design – Ernie Goyette

Published by Inspire Media, LLC
ISBN 0-9722332-0-2
Reprinted Network Leadership South Africa (Pty) Ltd
P O Box 13541, Mowbray, 7705

ACKNOWLEDGEMENTS

No book can be written without the enthusiasm and contribution of other people.

Thanks to all of the following:

Kim Mate for her support and editing.

Scott & MJ Michael for their example and integrity.

Suzanne Hubler for her inspiration.

I appreciate my years of association with the wonderful Independent Business Owners who have allowed me to pursue my dreams and use my unique ability.

DEDICATION

This book is dedicated
to the thousands of prospects
who have brought forward
interesting and tough questions
and left with no real answer,
therefore missing a great opportunity.
It is also dedicated to the thousands of IBOs
who so desperately wanted to answer
those interesting and tough questions
but lacked confidence and an EASY answer.

May you forever be armed!

CONTENTS

CONTENTS

CONTENTS

c

INTRODUCTION

You are about to become an ace through enhanced personal communication skills and greater influence. I'm impressed by your commitment to become better. You're part of an exciting new industry which will go down in history as the biggest, most successful entrepreneurial movement of our time.

I have been an entrepreneur for as long as I can remember. Most of my success has come from operating a home-managed e-commerce business. I started this business in my spare time and have encouraged others to do the same.

People often approach me with questions about the business. Our toughest job as independent business owners (IBOs) is responding to the questions people ask us. Too often IBOs miss the chance to create financial security for themselves because they didn't know how to respond to people's questions. Not only did they lack the right answers, but they also fell short in their communication skills. They lacked an understanding of subtle, but dramatically effective skills like listening, pausing, bridging, and modeling. These are the skills that build rapport and make you more assuring and credible. These are the skills we'll master together in this book.

The purpose of this book is to give you a knowledge base; a reference source if you will, to develop your skill sets and become a great

---

communicator.

When people are looking at our business concept for the first time, they will always have questions. If they don't have questions, they haven't understood the program. A question indicates that the prospect has been thinking about what's been said. It's a true sign of interest.

Imagine someone looking at a multi-million dollar idea for an hour. You turn to them and ask if they have any questions. They say no. That's a bad sign. A good sign is a question like, "Yeah, let me ask you this. How do the products get delivered?" Or, "Are sales involved in this?" Or, "Is this a pyramid?" Those questions are positives. They are an opportunity to engage in the next level of conversation, to educate the prospect. Remember, it is not the responsibility of the prospect to understand. It is the responsibility of the IBO to educate.

> **Key: It is not the responsibility of the prospect to understand. It is the responsibility of the IBO to educate.**

And it's not the responsibility of the IBO to understand. It's the responsibility of the upline to educate. And it's not the responsibility of the upline to understand. It's the responsibility of the leadership to educate.

I found that prospects asked the same questions over and over. I soon realized people didn't know how to handle these questions and objections. The reason they didn't know is that in most cases nobody had taught them! Approaching friends, family, associates and strangers can be one of the most difficult things a person does in our business. Yet, we expect new IBOs to 'go through the school of hard knocks' and learn the answers and communication skills on their own.

I say, "The heck with that!" Let's equip everyone who wants the answers. Let's empower every business owner with the best words, improved skills and heightened confidence immediately. With this book we can.

What people don't really understand is the difference between an objection and a rejection. An objection is a statement which disagrees, doubts or questions something that is being offered. The objection asks a question or states a position, but it's not a rejection.

A rejection, on the other hand, is a flat refusal to accept an idea or information. A rejection is a true no.

> **Key: There's a difference between an objection and a rejection.**

In every question, there is a question. We need to know where the prospect is coming from. We don't really know the underlying thoughts behind the question – are they looking for confirmation? Have they had a previous experience or are they merely looking for more information? We need to get more information from them before we can really answer the question.

One of the quotes I remember from a marketing class in college was, "If you want to know why John Smith buys what John Smith buys, you have to see the world through John Smith's eyes."

This quote is a great reminder to always put ourselves in the shoes of the person we are speaking with.

We then have to respond to these questions before we allow ourselves to get emotionally involved. If we interpret the question as a personal

> **Key: If you want to know why John Smith buys what John Smith buys, you have to see the world through John Smith's eyes.**

rejection, we either respond aggressively and fight, or we respond passively and flee. We need a high level of emotional intelligence to overcome the effect of an assumed rejection.

If we control our emotions when responding to objections and rejections, we can resist the negative feelings we associate with a prospect's question. Repeated practice eliminates the association of negative emotions with the process of contacting and showing the business plan.

Have you ever hung up the phone and thought, "I should have said...?" Have you ever been driving home from a meeting and given your steering wheel your best plan? The reason we all have these thoughts is that there is no pressure after the phone is hung up or the meeting is over!

What happens to your emotions when you hear, "I don't agree with that at all?" Your emotions go up! Further more, your intelligence goes down. Most people get tongue tied and flustered with objections because their emotions take over. So when the question is asked, your emotion rises and your ability to think clearly falters. It is not because you are dumb or weak. It is because you were conditioned that way.

The biggest benefit you will gain by reading this book is developing your 'emotional intelligence'. You will remain in control by learning to answer a question with a question. More importantly, you will eliminate the negative emotions associated with objections, you will listen to the questions, and you will hear what the prospect is truly asking.

> *You will remain in control by learning to answer a question with a question.*

I think when most people ask questions they are really saying, "Make me believe what you say is true". The only way to give them belief is if you believe. You can't just take these simple answers and recite them. You have to internalize the information and believe that it is true. Belief is one of those pass or fail things. You either have it or you don't. It's not enough to memorize the answers and expect success.

The thing I love about the conversation principles you are about to read is that they can all be learned. And what I like about "Confident

Conversations" is that it's a great first step to knowing more straight forward, honest answers which will ultimately give you a higher registration rate. You will register a certain number of people by responding with a question for a question. If you're able to give them an easy answer with a little bit of explanation, you will register more. And if you read "Further Thoughts" and give them a much deeper level of understanding, your registration numbers will be highest.

Use this book as reference material. It's designed to give answers to questions as they come up. The 38 questions and answers start in chapter 4 and are separated into categories – Who, What, When, Where, Why and How. The table of contents lists each question. Use this table to find the question and the question you can use in response. Learn the answers so well that you could repeat them in your sleep. When you can do that, there will be no emotion attached to the question or objection.

> *Learn the answers so well that you could repeat them in your sleep. When you can do that, there will be no emotion attached to the question or objection.*

I've also added a handy chapter at the end of this book to give you more variety and confidence as you respond to questions. This last chapter is titled 'The 21 Conversation Keys'. You'll love them! They contain great quotes, principles and nuggets you hear on audios while driving in your car. You wish you could pullover to write them down. Now you have them.

You'll notice some references to gender throughout the questions. Rather than the cumbersome he/she terminology, I've chosen to use one gender for each example. A prospect is he or she, but not both. You can use the terms interchangeably.

Don't lose sight of the fact that you can say all the right things, do all the right things, act all the right ways with the wrong person and they are not interested. It's not your fault. The prospect is just not interested. But if the prospect is asking questions or giving objections, they're really asking to be reassured. They're looking for more information. You have that information. Don't be afraid to use it.

Use this book. Abuse it. Rip the pages out of it and win with it. That's its ultimate design.

The founding philosophy of any referral-based business should be duplication. In other words, we teach teachers to teach teachers to teach. The genius of our industry lay in one word – duplication. Imagine having dozens, or even hundreds or thousands of business owners who have all mastered the principles and practices of confident conversations. Your business team will be unstoppable!

Let's master these skills together and set a wonderful example for those who watch and follow us.

I believe you are about to have a breakthrough in your business. The principles and practices in this book will work! They are proven. Now it's time to prove them to yourself. Your future is bright!

You can do it!

II. THE SEVEN CONVERSATION PRINCIPLES

It's important to realize how little of our communication is composed of words. In fact, according to some widely respected research conducted years ago by the Pacific Institute in Seattle, our communication is actually 93 percent non-verbal. That means that our words comprise only 7 percent of our total conversation!

If words represent such a small part of our communication, where does the other 93 percent come from? More than in any other way, people judge you and make decisions about how they think and feel about you based on your voice inflection, body language, appearance and listening skills.

Have you ever noticed how some people make the business look so easy? One day they were registered and it seemed the next day they were duplicating achievement with lots of new IBOs? How did they grow so fast when some of us seem to have so many struggles? Did they learn all the business strategies over night? Were they just lucky? My experience tells me they already had an understanding of the seven principles listed below. In other words, 93 percent of their effectiveness came from skills they had previously learned and then immediately leveraged those skills in our business.

CONVERSATION PRINCIPLE #1:
BE A GREAT LISTENER.

People generally talk much more than they listen. But the fact is, we learn only when listening. We learn nothing by talking. If you're going to succeed in any business, you've got to care about people. It's a matter of leadership. I'm sure you've heard the expression "People don't care how much you know, until they know how much you care." The best way in the world to show people how much you care— and the quickest way, too – is by listening.

I've heard over and over that the key to a successful business is to "find a need and fill it." The only way to find a need is by listening – really listening!

This isn't as easy as it might sound. Focusing on another person means shutting down everything on your own list, paying complete attention, and hearing every single word the other person says. Let me give you an example. A few years ago I recommended to an IBO (John) to record one of his 'one-to-one' business plan presentations so we could critique it together. A half hour into John's conversation, his prospect said, "I'm looking for a way to supplement my full-time income and make an additional $700 per month." Rather than using this information as power, John breezed right over the smaller income in the plan and focused on a six-figure income and total financial independence! We miss opportunity when we fail to listen.

> *The only way to find a need is by listening – really listening.*

Refusing to listen to people is the surest way of making others feel unimportant. Instead, make people feel important by listening with your ears, nodding with your head, and making eye contact. This lets people know that you are fully present with them and affirming their importance.

The best visual I can give you of a great listener are those mechanical flowers in a pot with a battery. They have a microphone and respond to sound. Have you ever seen one? They are hysterical to watch when you play music with a good beat because they actually 'dance' to the music they hear! My example might be a bit extreme, but our eye movement and head nods should be a direct response to what others are saying. Nodding shows agreement and creates a greater likelihood of a positive outcome.

In addition, the best listeners use the art of bridging. Bridging is a technique that keeps the conversation moving and avoids the situation where you might talk too much or your prospect talks too little.

Isn't it uncomfortable when you are showing a plan and your prospect responds with short, deliberate 'yes', 'no', 'kinda', 'not really' answers? You can avoid most of those situations by using simple, sincere phrases to keep them talking like:

So then...?

Meaning...?

For example...?

Therefore...?

Then you...?

Which means...?

When you use a bridge remember to first lean forward, stretch the last letter of the bridge, and then lean back and LISTEN.

CONVERSATION PRINCIPLE #2:
PEOPLE ARE MOST INTERESTED IN THEMSELVES.

One of the best selling books next to the Bible is 'How to Win Friends and Influence People' by Dale Carnegie. He writes "...a person's name is the most precious word in the English language." People are more interested in themselves than you! This is human nature. Simply recognize it and use it as power and skill with others. The most interesting subject in the world to others is themselves! Incorporate this principle by removing four words from your vocabulary – "I, me, my, mine." Then substitute those four words with one word –"YOU." For example use phrases like:

"You will benefit by…
"You get the advantage of…
"This will increase your…
"You can accomplish your goal of…

Another great way to instantly connect with others is to mirror and match their communication style. When you mirror and match the voice inflection, speed of speech, and body language of the person you're meeting with, you develop instant rapport – no matter what is being said. People are most open and comfortable with other people who are like them. Mirroring and matching is a practice whereby you observe and adopt some of the dominant characteristics of the person with whom you're speaking. Non-verbally, this behavior is saying, "I'm the same as you and we agree with each other and our attitudes."

If your prospect speaks very slowly and deliberately, you may need to slow it down to match their speed. Also, notice their vocabulary and integrate their words into your conversation.

For example, say you are meeting with a prospect at their home. Mr. Prospect leans back in his chair, puts a finger to his chin and says, "This looks interesting, but I'm always cautious at first," then leans forward and continues with, "but once I truly believe in something I become its greatest cheerleader."

A great way to respond would be leaning back, nodding and saying, "Interesting… I have always been the same way", then lean forward and say, "I've always believed the greatest sale you make is to yourself. I've become a real cheerleader in this industry because I did my homework and sold myself on the value of this idea."

Personally, I speak directly, quickly, and fairly loud. I also tend to use phrases like "I think," "I mean," and "right?" a lot in my conversation. I also use other key words like passion, purpose, empower, inspire, ignite, unstoppable and contribution among others.

If you came up to me, speaking quickly with passion and said, "Brad, this is great! I think we could ignite the hearts of others and build a team that would be unstoppable! Right? I mean, if we can connect people with what they are passionate about and build in a sense of contribution and purpose ..." I would be drawn to you. I would conclude you are a very intelligent, high-integrity person who's really up to doing great things in your life. I would like you and would respect you immediately, and I would want to spend time with you talking and sharing more ideas together. In fact, I'd be compelled to go into business with you!

> *People are like snowflakes: there are no two exactly alike.*

Mirroring and matching are the most powerful ways to have people on your side. This helps them be open and want to share with you who they are and where they want to go.

Remember, people are like snowflakes: there are no two exactly alike. If you talk about them, if you listen to them, if you model them, if you consider their desires, they will open up to you. They will come into partnership with you in a combined effort to achieve all your goals and theirs. That kind of powerful, inspiring relationship with others is the key to success.

CONVERSATION PRINCIPLE #3:
PAUSE BEFORE YOU ANSWER.

This gives others the impression that you have thought over what they said. It also gives you a moment to think of an appropriate response. People want to know their thoughts are real and valid. Most people jump into a conversation the moment there is a second of silence.

I was recently asked to do a business presentation to a group of college seniors at my alma mater San Diego State University. At the end of the event, the host asked if I'd be willing to do a Q & A session with the students. I obviously agreed and started taking questions from the audience. Wow! There were some very interesting, and very funny questions being asked. I wanted to make all their questions feel important and valued so as I responded to each one I would pause, and say something like; "Wow, what a great question...." Or "Hum, I've never been asked that before..." Or "Congratulations, that's an interesting perspective ..."

I call these phrases 'question acknowledgments'. They are especially useful on the phone when you are gathering your thoughts before responding.

CONVERSATION PRINCIPLE #4:
BE BRIEF AND FOCUSED.

The most interesting and compelling people to listen to are those who have concise, thought out statements or speeches. There is nothing worse than hearing someone run on and on and on and on. In fact some IBOs talk prospects into the business, and back out in the same conversation! One of the best lessons from this book can be your new learned skill of directed conversation.

> *Remember, it's best to leave a prospect 15 minutes before they wish you had!*

When you show the plan, do you wing it every time or do you have a pattern? If you want to have a big business, you should have a clear, concise, simple outline of your plan in your head.

Personally, my plan has a few major parts and some subpoints. These subpoints may be a quote, a short story, or a question I ask the prospect. My plan is memorized but natural. It is 'part of me'.

Just like a concert pianist doesn't have to 'think about' what keys his fingers will touch, I don't need to think about, stumble over, or contemplate every part of my plan. When you have an outline in your head, you become 'prospect focused' rather than 'me focused'. When showing the plan, challenge yourself to have more of a conversation, than a presentation.

For example, in my plan introduction I always tell a short two-minute story of the phone call I received to look at the business. This story is funny and a bit unusual. It creates a light atmosphere and puts people at ease right away.

Be brief and timely. Remember, it's best to leave a prospect 15 minutes before they wish you had!

CONVERSATION PRINCIPLE #5:
HAVE A GREAT FIRST IMPRESSION.

"You'll never get a second chance to make a first impression." Have you ever heard this from someone before? What they might not have known is that others will form up to 90 percent of their opinion about you in less than four minutes! Here are three ways to make that first impression golden:

<u>Have a great handshake</u>. Nothing is worse than shaking a wet noodle or even worse, having your fingers crushed by an overly dominant weight lifter! Have a firm handshake and adjust slightly to match the grip pressure of the other person.

<u>Use your smile power</u>! Studies show, the more you smile, the closer others are likely to stand next to you, the more eye contact they will give you, the more likely they will be to touch you, and the longer they will want to stay with you. In other words, smiling is great for your business and personal life. It shows others you are not a threat to them.

<u>Dress for success</u>. Clothing covers up to 90 percent of your body

and has a powerful effect on other people's perception of your trust-worthiness, reliability, expertise, authority, social success and business standing.

Here's what author Alan Pease says about dress, "The secret to appropriate business dress is in the answer to this question – How does your prospect expect you to be dressed? For you to appear credible, likeable, authoritative, knowledgeable, successful and approachable, how would you be dressed in their opinion? What suit, shirt, blouse, tie, skirt, shoes, watch, make-up and hairstyle would you be wearing? In their opinion – not yours."

CONVERSATION PRINCIPLE #6:
EVERY TIME YOU MAKE A POINT, TELL A STORY.

Every time you make a point, tell a story and every time you tell a story, make a point. The worst mistake IBOs make is *only* talking about facts, figures, details and statistics. Most prospects wake up the next morning and have forgotten 85% of the plan. People are impacted by benefits and value. The best way to communicate benefits and value to emotional beings is to speak emotionally. The best way to speak emotionally is with your personal story.

> *People don't remember facts, figures, details and statistics. People are impacted by benefits and value.*

Let's say for example that you were speaking to a prospect about attending a business presentation in your area.

You could say, "I'd recommend you attend the next business presentation at the Marriott hotel on September 27th; it's at 8:00pm. You'll learn a lot more about this business and meet lots of other people."

Or you could make it more personal by telling your story... "I remember looking at this idea for the first time, just like you are tonight, and really wondering 'could this idea work for me?' It wasn't until I attended a live presentation that I made a decision about my future. It was amazing! I met my other team members and saw people from 18 to 81 that were from all types of backgrounds: people who were school teachers, attorneys, construction workers and homemakers. The presenter was a young man who was 20 years younger than I, and was totally financially independent as a result of this idea. He answered most of my questions and made this business real to me. I'm so grateful today because I took a few hours out of my life to see if this idea could work for me."

Do you feel the difference? I've heard that "information tells, stories sell." Sell the business with your stories as you make your point, and make a point with your stories.

CONVERSATION PRINCIPLE #7:
BELIEVE IN WHO YOU ARE AND WHAT YOU HAVE.

Belief is everything in this business! It's that way in any business. No matter what career you choose, you must believe in what you're doing. You must believe in the company, their values and mission, their integrity, and you must believe in the people you're working with. There is no way to fake any of this. If you don't believe in what you're doing, you simply cannot be successful.

Have you met people in business whose words didn't convince you? A BMW salesperson who drives a Mercedes, or a personal trainer who takes different supplements from what he recommends to you? How many people are trading their time for money in jobs they can't stand? How persuasive, genuine, and honest is a person who doesn't believe in what they are doing?

Build belief in your business, and more importantly, build belief in yourself, by continuing to read books on success. I'd recommend you read at least one book a month. Then apply what you read! Remember the ONLY way to build self-esteem is through PERFORMANCE.

Also remember, belief is one of those 'pass or fail' things; you either have it or you don't. Belief is contagious and if you spread it, your business will grow like wildfire!

Belief in your business will come largely by associating with other business owners and attending training events. In addition, one of the first things I always recommend to IBOs is writing a summary of this opportunity in their own words and posting it where it can be seen everyday. It's a short paragraph that is your interpretation of the business. This paragraph will contain the words you will recite over and over in conversations with prospects. It will be used every time you show the plan, every time you follow-through. I'll even predict it's in your Diamond speech! It will be invaluable to you!

> **Belief is one of those pass or fail things; you either have it or you don't.**

You may describe the business as a massive 'affiliate program' on the Internet. Perhaps you prefer the term 'incentivized consumerism', 'referral commerce' or 'interactive commerce'. Throughout this book I use the term 'prosumer', which is defined as 'a profiting consumer in business'. It's always best to glean and identify yourself with the same terminology your upline team members use. My advice to you is don't waffle, don't keep switching, and don't change it every week based on the latest audio you've heard. Whichever term you use - and how you describe the business has to make sense! And when it does, you'll supercharge your accomplishment process. The more understanding you gain, the more inspirational power you have to influence others.

Here are three key ways we transfer our belief to others.
1. Through your words
2. Through your voice inflection
3. Through your body language

Some of these were discussed in Conversation Principle #2. I want you to consider them again. Now think about how others perceive your choice of words, voice inflection and body language. Think of it this way, if you heard 'your words' would you be compelled to act? If you heard 'your voice' inflection would you be inspired? If you saw 'your body language' would you be interested?

I often have IBOs leave themselves voicemails of their contacting lines and listen to themselves. Wow, this exercise can be revealing! When I talk to them later, I hear them say things like, "No wonder no one is interested in my business. I sound like a drone!"

These three forms of communication combine to form the skill we call "building rapport." When you learn the skill of establishing rapport with others, you will have developed infinite avenues for the experience and expression of business success, life success and success itself.

In essence, building rapport simply means establishing the most commonality and comfort possible in a relationship. Most human beings have a fascinating behavioral quality: We like people to like us. I know that's true for me. I would have a hard time warming up to someone who had just said to me, "You know,

> *"If you want to win a man to your cause, first convince him that you are his friend."*

Brad, I think you're crazy! I don't like you a bit. And besides that, you dress funny."

As Abraham Lincoln said, "If you want to win a man to your cause, first convince him that you are his friend."

We spend time with and feel comfortable with those people who share our interests and passions. Even people who have difficulty talking to strangers will do so easily if there is an obvious bond between them. They may both be riding Harley Davidson motorcycles, or they're both picking up golf clubs in baggage claim or wearing baseball caps from the same team.

Challenge yourself to get proficient with the seven conversation principles. Remember, it's not what you 'can' do in life that makes the difference; it's what you 'will' do. Knowledge itself is of no value. It is the use of knowledge that makes it valuable. These principles are your key to a better life, more friends, more success, and more happiness. Put them to work for you now. I hope you do.

II. THE GREATEST COLD CONTACTER IN THE WORLD

I'm sure most of you are reading this book hoping to get some great contacting lines. And while I will share some great examples with you, I want to remind you that 'Confident Conversations' is about giving you the skills to have confident conversations. The 'Seven Conversation Principles' in the previous chapter is the best advice I can give you for contacting strangers about your e-commerce business. The person who masters the Seven Principles will also master the art of being friendly, likable and relatable. In other words, you will become the best cold contacter in the world. Why? Because you don't contact strangers, you make friends first.

We personally register people to build a life for ourselves with this unlimited compensation plan. It's unlimited because you can register as many people as you want. However, your income will be directly related to your skill with people which, in turn determines your influence with them. Your ability to influence others will largely determine your effectiveness in registering and leading people into this great business.

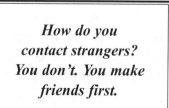

How do you contact strangers? You don't. You make friends first.

If you registered 100 front line IBOs and built strong business groups in just 20 of those, you would be one of the wealthiest people in America! Think about that. Is it possible? Sure it is. Consider other careers. Would it be possible for a real estate agent to sell 100 homes over their career? Or for a professional recruiter to place 100 executives? Or for a talented stockbroker to develop 100 clients? Of course.

Why don't people do it? I could probably give you 100 reasons, but all of them would eventually boil down to doubt and fear. I love what Henry Ford said, "I'm looking for men who have an infinite capacity to not know what can't be done."

When the dream is big enough the fear gets squashed! So really, what it boils down to is the size of your dream. What motivated you to read this book? I'll guess it wasn't just the 'information'. There was an 'inspiration' for something more. There was a picture in your mind's eye about how you want your life to turn out. Imagine how you would feel by grabbing this business by the tail and having wild success with it. Think of the freedom, adventure, fun, recognition, belonging, appreciation and wealth you would enjoy. It would be awesome!

> *When the dream is big enough, the fear gets squashed!*

Fear and doubt stifle your ability to accomplish your dreams. In the Bible it says: "He who doubts is like a wave of the sea, blown and tossed by the wind."

Fear is like an emotional roommate that lives with you day and night. It talks to you and manipulates you into side stepping anything uncomfortable. It speaks to you by saying, "You can't do that…" or "What will people think of you…" As fear speaks more, it eats away at your confidence and self-esteem. It convinces you not to move, not to reach out, not to try, not to believe, and not to act. It steals your life dreams right from under you.

Fear can be one of your most powerful inner enemies. It is a force that can sabotage your happiness. How does fear do this? It keeps you stuck in what's not working. It prevents you from growing. It creates separation between you and other people. It talks you out of your dreams. It keeps you stagnant, frozen, unable to become all you were meant to be. And sometimes it is difficult to recognize!

Right now in your life, there are things you want to do that you are not doing, changes you want to make that you are not making, conversations you need to have that you're not having, risks you want to take that you're not taking. Maybe you've been longing to do some of these things for weeks, months, even years, but you end up procrastinating. What's stopping you? Your fear. However, fear can also be a lot like fire.

Fire is harmless when it is controlled. It enables us to cook, it provides light and warmth, or it can set a romantic tone when contained in a fireplace and on a candle. Fear is the same. When your response to fear is uncontrolled, it can devastate. When your response is controlled, it can be used to motivate you, ignite you to action and bring you closer to your goals.

> *Maybe you've been longing to do some of these things for weeks, months, even years, but you end up procrastinating. What's stopping you? Your fear.*

My point is that fear in itself isn't good or bad. It can be either healthy or unhealthy. Fear is a tool, and like any tool that can be used to build or to destroy. The quality of how it serves you or undermines your efforts is up to you. It's just a choice.

You won't conquer your fear overnight, but you can start right here, right now. A Chinese proverb says, "The journey of a thousand miles begins with a single step." For those who decide to keep stepping forward, to risk, to grow, to change, will always face fear. Why? Because each time you want to grow, it involves moving into new territory, taking on new challenges. Isn't this great! Now you can give up trying to make fear go away. Fear and growth go together like a great meal at a restaurant comes with a gratuity. It's a package deal. The decision to grow always includes a choice of risk over comfort.

You will pay either way. The price of risk and fear is pennies on the dollar compared to comfort. Consider the price of getting to the end of your life, looking back and seeing... unique gifts and talents that were never used. Deep, intimate, gut wrenching conversations you never had. Rewarding goals you never set. Exhilarating adventures you never took. You're sitting in a recliner with a shriveled soul, and forgotten dreams. And you realize you missed your opportunities to be part of something bigger than yourself. You see the person you could have become, but did not. It's time to live, to wake up and do something. I heard it said, "A road called Someday leads to a town called Nowhere."

When it comes to our business, most people experience fear when contacting (prospecting) people. My first step through this fear was changing my approach with people. In other words, walking up to someone and asking them if they considered other ways of creating income scared the socks off me! In fact it still would. I learned a comfortable way to contact people through asking questions. It sounds like this:

"Do you like working here?"

"You must enjoy what you do?"

"Do you see yourself working in this industry forever?"

"Are you satisfied with your financial picture?"

"What do you like to do for recreation?"

"Where would you like to see yourself in five years?"

It's so simple! Just ask people questions. People will tell you why they would be interested in building a business of their own before you ask them!

REFERABILITY

The most powerful business strategy in the world is to be referable. Being referable means you are relatable, professional, friendly and comfortable to be with. When you have these qualities people believe in you so strongly that they want to tell others about you. They believe in you so much that they are very comfortable giving you plenty of names of people who may have an interest in your business. They will introduce you to those like themselves, or better. They actually clone themselves! Big companies pay millions in marketing to accomplish this and you can accomplish it with some basic habits. Here are four habits that Dan Sullivan, author of 'How The Best Get Better', recommends to successful entrepreneurs on how to become highly 'referable'.

1. Show up on time.
2. Do what you say.
3. Finish what you start.
4. Say please and thank you.

I know these four habits seem to be common sense, but a surprising number of people do not practice them. As a result these people are not referable. They may have brains, talent, charm, and experience, but they will never experience the 'snowball' effect of our business because nobody is comfortable referring them to others. These four habits demonstrate respect and appreciation thus avoiding feelings of indifference, arrogance, negligence, and sloppiness.

When you are referable, you can make dozens of simple phone calls and be well received. A referral phone call would start like this, "Hi John. This is Brad DeHaven. We haven't met yet but we have a mutual friend through _____ ."

If you are referable this phone call can make you millions in our business!

TEN PHRASES THAT MAKE THE DIFFERENCE

Here are some phrases you can use to ignite your conversations with prospects. I have personally made thousands of phone calls over the years and use these phrases repeatedly.

"Do you have a second, or am I catching you at a bad time?"

"If the money was right and it fit into your schedule, would you be open to looking at a business idea?"

"If I could show you a way to make some serious money with e-commerce, would you want me to tell you about it?"

"I'm looking to get this team assembled in the next two weeks."

"Between your contacts and my time and experience, we can both make a lot of money."

"I'd be willing…"

"I'd love to give you a shot at it."

"I'd welcome the opportunity to talk with you further about it."

"What nights this week do you already have commitments?"

"Hi" with a smile.

———————

FIVE MISTAKES TO AVOID ON THE PHONE

1. Always clear the time.

Great prospects (interested people) are often lost because you are calling at a bad time. Be sure to clear the time with a short opening comment like, "Do you have a second or am I catching you at a bad time?"

2. Don't send unnecessary literature or audios.

If a prospect requests literature, be certain they are a legitimate prospect and not someone simply trying to get rid of you.

3. Have a great telephone image.

The best way to improve how you sound on the phone is to tape your telephone conversations, play them back, and determine what areas need improvement.

4. Be prepared.

Write down and practice your phone script before you make calls. Also, clearly know your objective for the call.

5. Have a short compelling purpose for the call.

Develop interest by quickly introducing yourself, defining your purpose for the call and giving a benefit. Then immediately ask a question to engage your prospect in conversation.

Do you remember learning about the two types of energy in science class? Potential and kinetic. Potential energy is just that, potential. It just sits there, accomplishing nothing. Kinetic energy is energy in action. It's actually doing something. Kinetic energy is acting, talking and believing.

It's the same with these contacting phrases. 'Potential knowledge' does nothing. It doesn't speak or act when presented with an opportunity. 'Kinetic knowledge' on the other hand is active and making things happen, not just sitting there in your mind.

Charles Kettering said, "My interest is in the future because I am going to spend the rest of my life there."

Most importantly, you have been entrusted with a great gift. It is the gift of being able to empower others to live out a dream they may have given up on a long time ago. You also have a dream for yourself, for your family and those you love. Let this book be the beginning of reclaiming your destiny to become strong, confident and bold; to achieve your dreams, and to deliver the gift of freedom to others.

> *"My interest is in the future because I am going to spend the rest of my life there."*
> *-Charles Kettering*

The next six chapters contain 38 common questions people ask about our business. Each question is followed by three ways to respond. First, a question for a question. Second, an easy answer and third, further thoughts.

Remember that answering a question with a question keeps you in control of the conversation and gives you more insight to where your prospect is coming from. As you sharpen you conversation skills, you will find yourself combining words and phrases from all three types of responses.

EASY ANSWERS TO 38 TOUGH QUESTIONS

IV. WHO - WHO CAN DO THIS?

?QUESTION #1: I don't know if I could do this.

QUESTION FOR A QUESTION: What is it you're unsure about?

EASY ANSWER: I think you'd be great! In fact, you're already doing most of it! The only thing you haven't done is register as an IBO so you can profit from your purchases as a consumer.

FURTHER THOUGHT: We don't know if she can do it either. We need to know where this question is coming from in order to reassure the prospect of her potential for success. This prospect realizes she has no idea how to build this business. We make this assumption with all new IBOs – they don't know how to do this. If she knew how to do this, she'd already be doing it; and we would never have found her.

We're on a talent search. We are looking for people who have two things going for them. They either have the skills or they have the hunger to learn the skills necessary to be successful. Next we want to put the prospect into the personal and professional development system and see how quickly they are willing to learn this model. Can they do this? We don't know. We don't know if they're willing. Do they have a good attitude? Are they determined? Will they persevere? Do they have a good self-image? We don't know, but we can find out whether they have the interest to learn.

Anyone can do this. Prospects just need to hear you say that they can do this. Assure them with 'I think' statements, i.e., "I think you'd be great." "I think we can make a lot of money together." Then assure them you will be with them every step of the way.

?QUESTION #2: I don't think my partner would be interested.

QUESTION FOR A QUESTION: If he didn't do this with you, would you still be interested?

EASY ANSWER: Why don't you communicate your intentions and ask him to support you? I think we need to give him all the information so he can make an informed decision. I think your dreams and goals are worth it.

FURTHER THOUGHT: Many times I've shown the plan to one member of a couple. It's not always easy to get both partners together at the same time. The partner who hasn't seen the presentation is often resistant to change, especially when the explanation isn't clear. And there aren't many people who can take this information home and explain it well to their spouse.

There are two factors involved here. The first is that the spouse may be checking your prospect's true commitment. Most spouses want to support the other, but sometimes they're not sure of their partner's commitment to the business. And, they may be afraid of the amount of work required to support the process. Some positive, progressive action will often bring them around.

The second factor is that the prospect may be apprehensive about beginning a project they really don't know anything about. No one wants to start a new project by herself, and if the prospect perceives that her partner isn't willing to participate, she may be reluctant to do it alone. It's important to let your prospect know there are a lot of people building this business as singles. She doesn't need her husband to be involved in order to be successful. Her support team will make sure she gets what she needs.

?QUESTION #3: I don't know very many people.

QUESTION FOR A QUESTION: How many people do you think you'd have to know to be successful?

EASY ANSWER: You don't have to know a lot of people to make the business work. You can have great success with as few as three or four people who are interested.

FURTHER THOUGHT: People looking at the plan for the first time are unclear on the concept. The idea is so simple that they're looking for a catch. It's a really simple idea. Each one teaches one. We are all consumers and we profit from consuming through our independent business. We recommend the concept to other people who are looking for a way to improve their lives. The prospect doesn't have to know a lot of people to make his business a success. The prospect just has to know a few people who also know a few people who also know a few people. And, more importantly, the prospect needs to know that he's not finding these people alone – he has the support of a team of people committed to his success.

You could also say, "We have an advertising system that could help you discover people that would be interested". We start with a program called "making a list". It's the third step in the Pattern for Success. Who are your relatives? Who is on your Christmas list? Who is in your address book? Who do you know in this city? Who do you know...? The sources are limitless. Then, we finesse the list to find the people who are ambitious and who would relate to the support team member showing the plan.

QUESTION #4: I wouldn't want to take advantage of my friends.

QUESTION FOR A QUESTION: Will helping your friends make additional income be taking advantage of them?

EASY ANSWER: We wouldn't want you to take advantage of your friends either. In fact, we thought we would only approach the friends you felt could benefit from this idea. Why don't we just approach some of the people you feel could see the potential of the idea much like you have?

FURTHER THOUGHT: The person making this objection does not yet clearly understand the concept of the plan. It's important that she understands that the profit she receives from her own product volume - and her promotion of the idea to her friends, comes from the corporation, not from the friends with whom she gets into business.

Every person who becomes an IBO has their own primary motivating factor. We just focus on the things that would motivate their friends. Remember that if your prospect registers only one person, they make no money from that business. Registering people in width is what actually causes them to profit. In our business, you cannot make money from your friends unless you are actively pursuing a business network, building your own business and helping your friends to earn additional income.

The prospect also needs to know her friends are already consumers. And, just like her, they are already performing most of the activities required to build their own businesses. When we introduce the concept of becoming a Prosumer, her friends will appreciate the opportunity to receive the tax advantages of owning their own businesses and the unlimited income potential.

? *QUESTION #5:* I couldn't do what you do. I don't think I'd be as good as you.

QUESTION FOR A QUESTION: Why don't we find out what you're good at, and work as a team?

EASY ANSWER: If we work together, our training system will teach you what to do. You're already doing most of what it takes to be successful... you're just not reaping the benefits of being a Prosumer.

FURTHER THOUGHT: Everything in this business can be learned. We have a fantastic training system of books, audios and seminars. The prospect needs to participate in that training system to get the knowledge he needs. The skills of building the business come from practice. You have to be bad before you can be good.

Even better, how about the prospect using your skills to his advantage? I'll work with you. One of the reasons I contacted you is because there are some things you are really great at that I don't do well. I thought we could team up, and leverage each other's strengths. I am a great presenter, but I don't necessarily have the same convincing powers that you do. You seem to be a detail person where I'm not. That is what team building is all about. Identify the prospect's strengths and the source of his concern; then tell him you'll work together as a team.

The key to this question is to reassure the prospect that he doesn't have to build his business alone. He has the potential to learn the skills necessary to be successful. In fact, he already possesses most of the skills through other experiences – he just hasn't yet learned to apply them here.

My favorite quote on this matter is by Mother Teresa who said, "I can do things you can't do. You can do things I can't do, but together we can do great things!"

? ***QUESTION #6:*** Can I build this as a single?

QUESTION FOR A QUESTION: Do you think it takes building this business as a couple to be successful?

EASY ANSWER: This is a business that can benefit every household, no matter what the makeup of the people in that household. It's not gender specific; it's made up of all types of people from all types of backgrounds.

FURTHER THOUGHT: Sometimes prospects attend a seminar and see a lot of couples on stage, giving them the impression that you need to be part of a couple in order to build a successful business. As more and more singles are achieving success, this is becoming less of an issue. Perhaps your prospect should meet someone who is having success as a single.

Sometimes I ask the prospect, "Would you prefer to keep the money yourself or share it with somebody else?" The prospect always laughs, but my point is made.

One of the realities with singles is that they become so positive and so focused on their goals and dreams, they actually attract spouses too quickly. We can't keep them single very long! Certainly, if you would like to build it as a single you can.

Single males, single females, young couples, retired couples, couples with children, couples without children – anyone can build this business, and fit it into their approach and their lifestyle. As long as you consume replenishable products, and know others who do the same, you can build this business.

? ***QUESTION #7:*** Do I have to give up my friends?

QUESTION FOR A QUESTION: Wouldn't you like your friends to get involved?

EASY ANSWER: Of course not. But the more you learn about our business, the more you'll want your friends to be involved. For your friends who don't have an interest, that's great. We're not looking for "everybody". We're just looking for the "somebodies" who have an interest in profiting from their own business.

FURTHER THOUGHT: We're hoping the person you introduced this opportunity to has a circle of friends who are equally ambitious. We'd like to get them involved. In fact, that's the business of prosumerism – profiting consumers in business. Your prospect's friends all consume products. Would they like to make a profit from consuming and benefit from the tax advantages of owning a home-based business? So everyone is eligible, and I'd rather be in business with my friends than with strangers (although that's quite alright, too!)

You are an INDEPENDENT Business Owner (IBO). You can choose your friends. You can choose the people with whom you're associated. You're in charge.

I don't think choosing not to get involved has anything to do with friendship. Friends may or may not like or want to do what you do for a living, but that should not affect your friendship. What could affect a friendship is the manner in which the contact is made. This book will teach you how to make a contact, and that is something you can teach the prospect to do well. Be inviting, and let our business speak for itself.

EASY ANSWERS TO 38 TOUGH QUESTIONS

V. WHAT - WHAT IS IT?

?*QUESTION #8:* What is it?

QUESTION FOR A QUESTION: It's _____ (your industry term). Are you familiar with it?

EASY ANSWER: It's a brand new industry designed specifically for the Internet. I am part of a team of home-based entrepreneurs who teach _____. Are you familiar with it?

FURTHER THOUGHT: Simply put, we are Prosumers - profiting consumers in business. We have to treat this question as natural and expected - an information seeking question, not a challenge or an objection. People genuinely want to know more about what you're going to show them. But as we know, the concept is difficult to explain in a short answer. Here is where an advertising tool (audio, video, literature or CD-ROM) can really help a new IBO. It gives a prospect enough information before they create an uninformed opinion.

We ask, "Are you familiar with it?" knowing that the answer will likely be, "No". No matter what the answer, no or yes, our reply is, "Great! Let's get together and go over the details."

This question, more than any other, will be most frequently asked. Be prepared and have a good answer. This question will be best handled with your business summary discussed in chapter 2: Conversation Principle #7.

? *QUESTION #9:* Can you tell me more about it?

QUESTION FOR A QUESTION: Absolutely, I already have some information to loan you. What nights this week do you already have commitments?

EASY ANSWER: Absolutely. I already have some information to loan you.

Or… Absolutely, I've managed to have an expert come to my home on Thursday night to go over all the details.

FURTHER THOUGHT: The key word in your answer is 'absolutely'. This response ensures the prospect that you are willing and able to fully disclose the business concept. It says you are not dodging or evading their natural question of "Can you tell me more?" When we respond to this question with phrases like "I can't tell you more till we get together" or "It's like giving a hair cut over the phone" etc. it makes the prospect more suspicious and more likely to be negative about what you are offering.

Just like the previous question "What is it?", this question can be best handled with your business summary discussed in chapter 2: Conversation Principle #7.

?QUESTION #10: Is this Amway?

QUESTION FOR THE QUESTION: No this is not Amway, but what is your understanding of companies like Amway?

EASY ANSWER: No, this isn't Amway, but our administrator, Quixtar, has a partner store relationship with Amway along with about 200 other companies. Quixtar is a subsidiary of Alticor Inc., as is Amway Corporation, and the two separate companies often get confused.

FURTHER THOUGHT: Many people simply use the term 'Amway' as a generic term for the MLM industry. For many people, Amway means the same as Herbal Life, Avon, etc. because Amway has always been the industry leader.

Your answer to their question depends on their answer to your question. It would be an error to assume that the question has a negative connotation. The person asking this question has a perception about Amway, and you need to find out where they're coming from.

The question might be a way for the prospect to orient her thoughts. Adult learners tend to want to link something new to what they already know. A new concept is scary – we all need to categorize, or put a frame around an idea so we know where to file it in our brain.

The question may indeed be a request for information about a link between Amway and our business. I always explain that our business team leads the industry. Prosumers are profiting consumers in business. Our source of consumable products is the Quixtar Corporation. Quixtar is a subsidiary of Alticor Inc., which is a global enterprise doing business in manufacturing, marketing, logistics, and product and business development. Quixtar is a North American web-based business, and Amway is a traditional direct sales opportunity that is global in scope.

QUESTION #11: Is this a network marketing business?

QUESTION FOR A QUESTION: What is your experience with network marketing?

EASY ANSWER: This is a brand new industry designed specifically for the Internet. It has a referral-based component to it known as affiliate marketing. Big companies like Wal-Mart, American Airlines and Amazon are all using affiliate programs.

FURTHER THOUGHT: You have to place the question in the right context so you can give them the right content. "Network marketing, sounds like you are familiar with it." "What do you know about networking?" Once you've heard their thoughts, you can handle the question in the right context.

Our industry stems from an original 1980's concept, which was known as network marketing. Today, a more contemporary term would be an 'affiliate program.' Quixtar.com is actually a gigantic web of on-line affiliates who pay commissions to IBOs for their purchases and referred purchases. Furthermore, our business teaches how to organize and duplicate a business system through audios, books and training seminars.

This question may also come in the form of a question about multi-level marketing. Our business uses a multi-level structure because it is the most successful structure in the world. Technically, this is a multi-level marketing plan, but the term "multi-level" embraces too many other models that do not resemble our business in any way. Our edge is to reposition ourselves in the marketplace, and draw comparisons to other well-known companies like Wal-Mart, American Airlines, and Amazon.com that have affiliate programs (pay commissions for purchases).

QUESTION #12: This looks a bit like a pyramid to me.

QUESTION FOR A QUESTION: What's your interpretation of a pyramid?

EASY ANSWER: Most conventional businesses have some form of hierarchy. The police, the school system, the church, IBM, and Coca Cola are all examples of hierarchical businesses. It makes sense that ours would be similar.

FURTHER THOUGHT: I explain our business as a collection of work groups or teams. If a prospect is asking about a pyramid, they are skeptical, and are attributing negative characteristics to the referral component of our plan. The only connotation of a pyramid in this context is something illegal, and we have to dispel that right away. There is nothing illegal about our business.

Most conventional businesses are shaped like a pyramid. For example, the government, the church, the police department, and the educational system are all pyramids. In a pyramid you cannot pass the people above you. In our program, there is no limit to how high you can go. In fact, someone who joins our business tomorrow could eventually pass up the highest earner in our business.

In 1979, the U.S. Federal Trade Commission ruled on the legality of the compensation plan on which the Quixtar business is based. Unlike illegal business plans, our business does not require a large, initial fee, investment, or purchase of inventory. Quixtar does not pay a bonus unless products are purchased and sold or used, nor does it pay a bonus for the mere act of registering another person into the business. We do not require IBOs to stock and maintain expensive inventories. There are no minimum order requirements.

Affiliation with well-known corporations such as Microsoft, IBM, Office Max, Panasonic, GE, Ralph Lauren, Sony, Proctor-Silex, and Kellogg's should reassure a prospect.

EASY ANSWERS TO 38 TOUGH QUESTIONS

VI. WHEN - WHEN CAN I DO IT?

?QUESTION #13: I'm too busy. I don't have time to take on anything else.

QUESTION FOR A QUESTION: If it were worth it financially,
could you make the time?

EASY ANSWER: I know how you feel. I felt the same way, but what
I found is that while no one has the spare time to do this, many people prioritize their time because this business is worth it.

FURTHER THOUGHT: Another question related to this is "How
much time does this take?" That question is a little more positive, but
the answers to both are the same.

The time it will take is relative to the size of your goals. You can
put in a few hours a week or you can put in a few hours a day. It
depends what you are looking for.

Investing time is like planting seeds. The more seeds you plant, the
more exponentially the crop grows. How much time are you willing
to put into your future? It's up to you.

Will you have more time in five years? We'd like you to work
your way out of work. We'd like to see this as your career, to choose
it as your profession, so eventually you can be free full time. There's
no value in giving your time to working overtime at a job.

One of the great things about a team system like ours is you can
leverage the time of your team as well. This prospect can have their
active support team members make phone calls, show the plan, etc.
With a prospect who is truly short on time I like to use the phrase,
"With your contacts and my time and experience, I think we can
make some money together."

People make time for the things they want to do. What people are
really saying is: You haven't convinced me that this is worth my time
or that the reward is big enough to take priority over something else.
Build their dream and make it worth their while.

QUESTION #14: Isn't the market already saturated?

QUESTION FOR A QUESTION: Saturation is our goal. What percent of the market do you want?

EASY ANSWER: Just a fraction of one percent of the population is involved in our business. We can't even keep up with the birth rate, let alone saturate the marketplace.

FURTHER THOUGHT: Saturation is not our fear; it's our goal. We are actually looking to impact as many people as we can here in North America. Right now, there are only about 700,000 IBOs, roughly 1/4 of one percent, in the United States (100,000 in Canada, or 1/3 of one percent). At 0.25%, we are nowhere near saturation! Our goal is to have 10% to 20% of the population of North America involved in our business.

The prospect that fears saturation worries about finding people. Here are some simple numbers: approximately 100 people using 100 PV in each of three legs - or a total of 300 people would net approximately $75,000 per year. In order to make a solid income, you really only need a few people in a properly structured business.

Every day, more people turn 18 years of age and become eligible to create their own futures through this business than are currently signing up every month in our industry. We're a long way from saturation of the population! The growth figures indicate we'll never get there.

EASY ANSWERS TO 38 TOUGH QUESTIONS

VII. WHERE - WHERE CAN I DO IT?

?QUESTION #15: Do I have to go to all the meetings?

QUESTION FOR A QUESTION: What are your thoughts about the meetings?

EASY ANSWER: No, you can do whatever you want; it's your business. But success in any new endeavor will require training, teamwork, and association. We use the meetings as our office where you receive the latest information and can connect with your support team. Later on, you can bring your new people to a meeting so they can get the same perspective.

FURTHER THOUGHT: Initially, the prospect is thinking about the time commitment, and whether she has to watch a presentation every week. She doesn't understand that the meetings are both a training ground and an office.

As she starts out, the prospect gets a lot of her information from the audios and books. As time progresses, she will find that the meetings can give her the next level of insight into how to build her business successfully. They are actually the most efficient way to use her time. She can meet new people, connect with others on her team and set up meetings to work depth. She can watch her support team and see how they direct their focus and follow through with people. And she can learn new techniques of presenting the IBO Plan.

I always say, "You can rent office space and hire an entire consulting staff to train you and your team for the cost of a sandwich!"

The meetings are a way to help others understand what you have seen. We strive to bring new people to hotel presentations so they can see success and catch the excitement of a large gathering of people all focused on a common goal. You can't buy that kind of excitement, but it's worth a lot of money for your business.

And let's not forget the power of association. The meetings create an environment for people to associate with like-minded people – optimistic, focused, excited, and hopeful. Emotions are infectious! Research shows it only takes thirty seconds for someone with a strong attitude to infect others with that attitude. We want to associate with people who have a great attitude.

This question can be asked slightly different with, "I'm self-motivated. I don't need to go to the meetings." This question is similar and can be answered like this, "I know you're a self-starter. That's why I contacted you. The meetings are designed as your office and a training ground for new people you introduce to the business. They are a way you can work smart with your time."

Motivation comes from inside. Most people lack success because they're not in an environment where their dreams are encouraged, where attitudes are positive, and where people have hope. We have to create a rich environment that enables people to draw upon those internal qualities they need to be successful. The meetings and seminars stimulate people who live and work in negative, de-motivating environments.

Even though this prospect may be a self-starter and have the right environment to flourish in, the people to whom he introduces the business may not be. In fact, most people interested in our business aren't in the right environment. That's why they're looking for something more in their life.

Eventually, this prospect will come to understand the meetings are for new people and for people who are building their business with new people.

?QUESTION #16: I live downtown. Doesn't a business like this work best in more rural areas?

QUESTION FOR A QUESTION: Do you feel this business wouldn't be successful in a city environment?

EASY ANSWER: Whether it's New York City or a rural farm community in Idaho, we are seeing success. Growth and excitement are determined more by leadership than climate or demographics. The reason I contacted you was because I feel you have the leadership qualities to build a strong business in _____ (their area).

FURTHER THOUGHT: This business can be built wherever you are living. There is success in Trinadad, Puerto Rico, Hawaii, California, and New York. Just to name a few places.

Look at it this way. Two people buy exercise bikes. One person loses weight, and the other doesn't. Was one of the bikes defective? Of course not. One person used the bike and the other person did not. The same is true with this business. This is a business you can develop, teach, and duplicate in any area and in any environment as long as you talk to people about it!

You may also get a similar question that may sound something like this, "I'm moving across the country next month. Can I build this business there?" Remember, you can build this business anywhere in North America.

EASY ANSWERS TO 38 TOUGH QUESTIONS

VIII. WHY - WHY WOULD I DO THIS?

QUESTION #17: I don't really like all the hype.

QUESTION FOR A QUESTION: I understand. How do you feel about educational and motivational environments?

EASY ANSWER: That's the beauty of this business – there's something to suit every kind of personality. Rather than teaching this business in a stale environment, we make learning fun. I hope you don't see our excitement as insincere hype.

FURTHER THOUGHT: Everyone needs to feel good about their decision to become business owners. We need to create an atmosphere of excitement to maintain their enthusiasm about their business. Some people confuse hype with insincerity. It's important to understand that people have different styles of expression.

It's hard to curb enthusiasm when people are making some significant changes in their lives, their finances, and their hopes and dreams. It's important not to take offense to other people's way of expressing their enthusiasm about their business.

Sometimes the prospect's comment is associated to their personality temperament. The "outgoing" personality is likely to love all the excitement. They are outgoing and vivacious, and probably live a life of hype. The "detailed" personality is calmer, more reserved, taking an analytical approach to the business. Feelings are less important to the detailed person. If you understand the personality of the person asking the question, you can respond in a way that will meet their needs. Don't let their personality style be a barrier to the true opportunity.

Change the word "hype" to "excitement". Motivational environments are supposed to have excitement. Emotion is infectious, and decisions are based on emotion, not on logic. In a motivating environment, people will make decisions and commitments to building a future for themselves and their families. These prospects, even though they think they don't need excitement, will find people who do.

QUESTION #18: This sounds materialistic.

QUESTION FOR A QUESTION: If you happened into a lot of wealth due to your hard work, what would you do with it?

EASY ANSWER: The success from this business can be interpreted as material, but much of the success is displayed in the form of personal development and quality of life. When you have built your business and have generated income, you can choose what you want to do with it.

FURTHER THOUGHT: It sounds like this prospect has lost her ability to dream, and to have hope for her future success. We need to give her permission to allow herself to hope that there is something more she can do for her future. Most people who talk about materialism are not in a position to choose where their money goes.

Everything we would like to do, even the non-materialistic things, takes money. If you have enough money, you can help a lot of people. You can endow a museum or a gallery. You can send out a missionary, or become one yourself. You can travel the world. You can fund a scholarship. You can support medical research. There's no limit to what you can do if you have enough resources. When you have everything you need, money becomes a non-issue, and the money then can become a tool for philanthropy.

Remember the primary motivating factors. Ask the prospect, "What caused you to think about doing a business like this?" What is your primary motivating factor? If it isn't money, and it isn't material things, what does make you go? Personal and professional development? Leaving a legacy? Helping others? Unfortunately, the only way some people define success is through material things. If we don't demonstrate wealth through material things, those people won't believe that the business works.

QUESTION #19: What are my odds of making it in this business?

QUESTION FOR A QUESTION: What are your odds of making it without it?

EASY ANSWER: The chances of success are the same for everyone who starts this kind of independent business. Our business is structured to provide a level playing field for everyone. Your odds of success are directly related to your perseverance and your willingness to learn.

FURTHER THOUGHT: The prospect asking this question is really asking you to tell him that he can do it. He's looking for encouragement. He's not really looking for a specific answer about the law of averages. He's looking for confidence. If you respond with the "I think..." attitude: I think you'd be great at this. I think we can build a huge business... you can help develop a great commitment from this person. Make him feel like the odds are in his favor with your support.

It's dangerous to focus on the odds, or the averages. 95% of the population is average. The 5% who aren't average are the ones who are successful in life. This is a business idea that costs several hundred dollars with the earning potential of several million dollars in a 2-5 year program. Your prospect has a support team who knows how to build a successful business, and who is committed to helping him succeed.

The odds are often against the most successful people. We see examples of this all the time in the world of business, in the world of athletics, i.e, the Olympics. What counts is determination, vision and belief. Life is about overcoming the odds. Believe in your prospect, and he will believe in himself.

QUESTION #20: My friends and family will probably not approve.

QUESTION FOR A QUESTION: Have you approached your family with this type of situation before? What happened?

EASY ANSWER: I'd be happy to present the idea to them very professionally. Perhaps if they saw it the same way you did, they'd feel differently.

FURTHER THOUGHT: Perhaps this prospect has already attempted other ways of improving his lifestyle with little success. Family members, including spouses, can often be hard on the person who has tried and failed. And the opinions of our families are important to us. We often see ourselves the way others see us.

If a man's friends and family do not approve of this business, there are probably other things that he does now of which they don't approve. As individuals, we each have free will. We are not necessarily looking for others to approve so much as to understand.

We don't ask our neighbors if we should get married. We don't ask our parents whether we should have children. Your family and friends do not pay your bills. Their opinions didn't determine the work you do or where you work or what your hobbies are. You, and only you, are responsible for the decisions you make.

Sometimes the lack of approval is a result of misunderstanding the business concept. If his friends or family saw the same presentation, they might understand more clearly the concept of our business, and be more supportive of this prospect and his business.

Make sure your prospect has done his 'due diligence' and understands what he is getting involved with. This is a great idea. Our business is the trend of the immediate future - it's starting right now! We believe that, and we have to assure this prospect that he can believe it, too.

?QUESTION #21: I'm not interested.

QUESTION FOR A QUESTION: Thank you for being honest. Which part are you not interested in?

EASY ANSWER: Thanks for your honesty. Allow me to ask you a quick question.
1. Would it be worth 20 minutes of your time to know more about what you are turning down? There could definitely be some profit in it for you.
2. I'm looking to have my team assembled by the end of the month. Do you know anyone open to looking at a part-time, home managed business and earn $___?

FURTHER THOUGHT: The answer to this question will be different depending on when you hear it – before the plan or after. If this prospect has just seen the plan in its entirety and they are not interested, no big deal. Keep showing the plan to others and have the law of averages work for you. However, always remember to ask for a referral or if they would be interested in becoming a client or member. If you hear this objection before showing them the plan, then they are unwilling to look at a new concept for whatever reason. They may have one of the many other objections we've talked about – too busy, fear of failure, etc. So, they play it safe by not listening to the idea at all.

We can only respond with questions that focus on the four main motivators – time, money, security and choices. What is it that you are not interested in? Enough money to meet all your needs? The goods and services delivered to your door? The help of your support team? The personal and professional development? The time flexibility?

Try to get them to be specific about what they're <u>not</u> interested in. Their answer will give you an opportunity to respond appropriately. Remember to use the primary motivating factors, and the benefits of an ideal business. Invariably the prospect will identify one of the other issues identified in this book, and you can lead to the appropriate answers.

It's impossible to be uninterested in something you haven't seen. It is possible, however, to be uninterested in what you have seen. That's the purpose of advertising/screening tools. Your goal is to find out which category the prospect falls into, respond appropriately and move on.

QUESTION #22: How much money are you making?

QUESTION FOR A QUESTION: How much would you like to make?

EASY ANSWER: The money I make is right on track with my performance. My personal goal is to make $____, but I can introduce you to some of my team members who are making great six figure incomes.

FURTHER THOUGHT: In answering this question we're often tempted to embellish the truth. I say, tell the truth. There's nothing wrong with saying I am a 1,000 pin and I make $200 a month. I'm just getting started.
Here are some generic answers that anybody can use to position themselves:

1. "For the work and effort I've put in, I'm pleased."
2. "Enough to keep me interested."
3. "I'm going through training right now and have developed a plan to replace my full-time income."

Make no mistake. I don't want you to lie, exaggerate, or manipulate. If people ask how much money you make, you could say, "Well, I'm on track for the work I've put in. I made $63 last month. The good news is that I'm focused on my goal to make $6,000 a month and I know exactly what I need to do to achieve that. My income is based on the extent of width and depth I've developed in my business. The income in this business is directly related to structure. I'd be willing to explain it to you."
If they ask how many people you have registered, tell them. If

you've been in the business for a few years, but just recently started to really apply yourself, it may be appropriate to say, "I'm really now just getting started and I've already registered two people". If you lie to people, they'll know anyway. The prospect will appreciate your honesty and is more likely to trust everything else you say.

QUESTION #23: Will getting involved in this affect my unemployment/social assistance check?

QUESTION FOR A QUESTION: Is your unemployment check sufficient for the life-style that you want?

EASY ANSWER: I'm sure you're not on unemployment/social assistance by choice. I'd like to help you build your income to the point where you no longer need that check.

FURTHER THOUGHT: This prospect's primary motivating factor is security. He needs to know his current income isn't threatened by a new business activity. In Maslow's hierarchy of needs, he is at the bottom, focused solely on survival. Sometimes we think that unemployment or social assistance is a choice, and it can be. But more often, it's a trap that people can't get out of.

Being on any kind of social assistance can be discouraging. We have to help the prospect see that becoming an IBO is the way out of an impossible situation. He is trying to work his way out of work. The government will not penalize him for profiting in his own business. They'll take his unemployment check and as his income goes up they will balance the assistance against the income. Hopefully, he'll be making so much money he won't even need unemployment. The objective is to hand him back his self-esteem and confidence so he is in control of his own life and his own future.

We hope to develop enough skill sets in the prospect so that he will not be unemployed. He will actually be successful enough to find a new career with a new skill set. We believe that people who join our personal/professional development program enhance their personal lives, regardless of the level at which they begin.

? *QUESTION #24:* I've seen this before.

QUESTION FOR A QUESTION: What exactly did you see before?

EASY ANSWER: I had, too. But I never saw it with the same professional and profitable approach our team uses with this industry.

FURTHER THOUGHT: Your response will also depend on when you hear this objection. Is it before or after the plan. If I heard this objection before the plan, my gut feeling would be, 'If you haven't seen it from me, you haven't seen it!' I don't always say this because it can come across as bullish or rude. We have to ask questions about this response to find out what the prospect really thinks. Did she see our plan before and reject it? Was she interested but the timing wasn't right? How long ago did she see it? Were there some differences?

If you hear this after the plan say, "Great! What did you like best about it?" By focusing on what he liked, we can emphasize cutting-edge team we are part of. This prospect is seeing evidence of the current and continued change which makes the business better today.

It may be that there are major differences between what she is seeing now and what she saw a long time ago. It may be that she saw something similar but it wasn't our program. Whatever the response, what the prospect liked best should be the focus of the next part of your discussion.

? *QUESTION #25:* I can't afford it right now.

QUESTION FOR A QUESTION: In the mean time, why don't we start your training and you can save up the money to get started. How does that sound?

EASY ANSWER: You don't have to have an IBO number to get started learning the business. If you think this is something you'd like to do, why don't we show the program to a couple of your friends? Let's take the business for a test drive. You can get registered later.

FURTHER THOUGHT: We need to focus this person on the 'Why' of the business. The old adage, "Where there's a will, there's a way", applies here. If the prospect has a strong enough reason to participate, he'll find a way to do it. We build him a dream.

I find it interesting that we can always find the money to do the things we want, or to handle the emergencies of life. What this person is really saying is that he doesn't have enough belief in his ability to have success in this business to rearrange his financial priorities.

We therefore have to help him to feel successful. I say, "Here's what we'll do. Why don't we give it a test-drive? If you do come across some people with interest, we'll re-evaluate whether or not it is worthwhile for you to spend the money. Give the business a test-drive." If he gets three people interested, you'll be amazed at what he will reprioritize. Everybody has the money. People just don't have the focus.

?QUESTION #26: I was in a business like this a long time ago. What's different about this?

QUESTION FOR A QUESTION: What did you like about the concept then?

EASY ANSWER: Everything! With the introduction of e-commerce and a virtual office, just about everything is different. The entire concept has been given a face-lift. We are part of a cutting-edge industry that is about to sweep North America.

FURTHER THOUGHT: This prospect is going to be very excited about what you have to show her. This business was launched in 1999 and is a whole new industry. The easy answer to this question is, "Everything"! Use it!

This is a completely different model from the one with which the prospect is familiar (network marketing, Amway, Herbal-Life, etc.). There is a broader product line, more companies, and a professional training system. The list of innovations is endless.

Our newly defined business model is a key component of what separates us from the past. It streamlines the whole process of operating a home-managed business. The Independent Business Owner can focus on three aspects: purchasing products on-line from his own store for delivery to the location of his choice, making a profit on the movement of product through his business, and recommending the process to other people.

What's changed? Everything!

QUESTION #27: I am involved with or thinking about another network marketing company that has worked really well for some of my friends.

QUESTION FOR A QUESTION: I understand. What's the bottom line for you to make a decision?

EASY ANSWER: What do you hope to achieve in developing your own business? Let me give you enough information about this concept to help you compare the two. Then you can make an informed decision about your future.

FURTHER THOUGHT: This person is in the looking window. He meets all the criteria of a good candidate for your business. However, he has a strong connection with another opportunity because of his relationship with his friends.

Relationship marketing is the context within which our business operates. People are loyal to a variety of businesses and services because of the connections they have made with the service providers – the clerk behind the counter at the variety store, the bank teller who always has a ready smile, and the courier who always asks about your family. Someone looking at the opportunity to participate in a successful business venture with friends would have to have a strong reason to go in a different direction.

Think about your own situation. You have the best business opportunity in the world. Would you give it up to go to another entrepreneurial environment?

The best thing to do for this prospect is to encourage him to do his research, and attend the next event where he can meet other people. The more he researches the information and the team, the more confident he will become, which increases the likelihood of his success. The prospect will not join us unless they are convinced it is a better opportunity than the opportunity their friends are offering.

EASY ANSWERS TO 38 TOUGH QUESTIONS

IX. HOW - HOW CAN I DO THIS?

QUESTION #28: Do I have to sell?

QUESTION FOR A QUESTION: Do you like to sell?

EASY ANSWER: Yes – You'll love this! No – You'll love this!

FURTHER THOUGHT: We are profiting consumers in business. We buy products from our own store, receive profit on those purchases and tell other people what a great idea it is. Ultimately, we are selling ideas and products.

The majority of the population does not like to sell. Why? We're all afraid of rejection. That's the beauty of this book! If you practice these questions and answers often enough, you can eliminate the emotion behind the question, and the answers will come naturally and confidently.

But this prospect is not yet at that stage, and may be hesitant to take on something she feels uncomfortable about. We need to reassure her that selling is not the major activity of the business; at least, not selling as she probably defines it.

In fact, much of what we do in our day-to-day lives is selling. When we recommend a good movie or an excellent restaurant, we have "sold" the movie or the restaurant with our recommendation. That's the kind of selling we do.

If I talk excitedly about something I believe in and something I have achieved some success with, is that selling?

? *QUESTION #29:* This would be a conflict of interest with my employer.

QUESTION FOR A QUESTION: How would this be a conflict?

EASY ANSWER: Let's find out which portion of the business is in conflict, and let's work around it.

FURTHER THOUGHT: There is no doubt that some of the activities in our business could be a conflict of interest for the prospect. For example, if someone were to work for a company that manufactures vitamins and herbals, it may be a conflict to promote the sales of a competing brand of product through the prospect's own business. One way to handle such a conflict would be for the prospect to put her business in her spouse's name.

There are some occupations that closely guard their client lists. That's not a problem for us because we advocate refraining from business activity during the time you spend at work. It's understandable that a client list is sacred in order to protect the client.

Many insurance reps have been told they can't have a secondary income because it's a conflict of interest. An insurance person is in people's homes. He or she builds a relationship. There's a trust factor. A person could tell the prospect – "Well, if you're not interested in insurance, how about this other thing?" To me that's an absolute lack of integrity. If your company says don't contact anybody, then don't contact anybody. Don't touch your client list.

However, for an employer to take charge of all the things in your life – that's bold. Your employer actually forces you to agree that for the fixed amount of money he gives you, he controls you seven days a week, twenty-four hours a day, three hundred and sixty-five days a year. They actually top you out, max you out, and make you sign it, and you're OK with that? What does the future hold for you if you know you are capped and controlled?

QUESTION #30: I don't want to use my credit card over the Internet.

QUESTION FOR A QUESTION: It sounds like security is a concern for you?

EASY ANSWER: The Quixtar website has the finest data bit encryption code for security purposes. That's the same level of security used by the banks and trust companies on the Internet.

FURTHER THOUGHT: A person worried about this issue is new with Internet technology. It's understandable that someone would be hesitant using a service she is not entirely familiar with. She needs to be reassured that her credit and her funds are not in jeopardy by completing financial transactions over the Internet.

The encryption code used by Quixtar is the same level of security used by banks and trust companies in banking transactions. I wondered about that issue, too. What I found was that the likelihood of being defrauded over the Internet is extremely small. You are much more likely to have your credit card compromised by an attendant at a gas station than you are to be victimized over the Internet.

However, there are other options available. The person who is hesitant about Internet purchases by credit card can complete any transaction by telephone. Telephone ordering can also be used by those IBOs who do not yet have Internet access.

QUESTION #31: I don't have a credit card.

QUESTION FOR A QUESTION: What are your views about owning a credit card?

EASY ANSWER: Quixtar has several payment options available. We'll find the one that is best for you. You can use a check, debit card or we can arrange for a bank draft. It would be worth it to get a credit card to build your business because it makes transactions easier.

FURTHER THOUGHT: There are three issues here. The first is that the prospect may have principles about using credit. In that case, I would try to dispel his fears about incurring debt through the use of a credit card. The credit card is a tool for efficient ordering. It is not intended for extension of credit. In fact, I advocate the immediate paying of the credit card balance. I teach my IBOs to write a check to their credit card or access their on-line banking immediately after using their card to make a Quixtar purchase. An immediate payment accumulates no interest on the card.

If the prospect simply has never applied for a card, he may want to consider getting a credit card for business purposes only. I recommend the Quixtar Visa, which can be used to pay for on-line or telephone purchases through Quixtar. The Quixtar Visa has the added benefit of the accumulation of PV and BV on the dollar values charged to the card. Imagine – PV on your PV!

The third issue may be that the prospect is unable to acquire a credit card due to a lack of, or an unstable credit rating. In which case there are other options. They can order by mail and send in a check, set up a bank draft authorized through the upline Platinum IBO, or obtain a checking account with a Visa debit card that draws from their checking account.

Simply knowing these options are available will usually be enough to remove a barrier for the prospect.

?QUESTION #32: I'm not good at going up to people and asking them for something or selling them something.

QUESTION FOR A QUESTION: I understand. Is that your view of this business?

EASY ANSWER: Our business is all about buying products from your own store, receiving profit on those purchases, and telling other people what a great idea it is. We don't want you to approach anyone about this idea until you feel you understand it. The purposes of our advertising/screening tools are to help you screen the people who would be interested. Let the tools do the work for you.

FURTHER THOUGHT: The prospect making this statement is afraid of being rejected. To overcome our fear of what the other person will say, we should overcome the emotion we attach to their response.

The funny thing is, we're not good at asking people for something either. That's why our Business System is so effective. Our system takes care of the impression that we're selling something – we're not! We are sharing the best business idea in existence!

That's the purpose of our advertising materials, tapes, videos, CDs and brochures. We're not trying to sell anything. We're just asking a bright, ambitious person to take a look at this information. They can say yes or no.

Reassure the prospect that in addition to the tools, she will also have the help of her support team to introduce this concept to the people she knows, and to show her how she can be most effective in communicating the idea to others.

**?*QUESTION #33:* Do I have to wear a coat and tie every time I meet with a prospect?

QUESTION FOR A QUESTION: Do you wear a coat and tie at your job now?

EASY ANSWER: You can wear whatever you want. It's your business. However, I would recommend you dress to your level of commitment. Let your image match the level of professionalism you wish to portray.

FURTHER THOUGHT: Don't necessarily be influenced by the trend of many companies that have abandoned the coat and tie. Being professionally dressed will say a lot to your friends about your commitment. Studies show people actually respond differently based on what they are wearing.

Clothing covers up to 90 percent of your body and has powerful effect on other people's perception of your trustworthiness, reliability, expertise, authority, social success and business standing.

Here's what Alan Pease says about dress, "The secret to appropriate business dress is in the answer to this question – How does your prospect expect you to be dressed? For you to appear credible, likeable, authoritative, knowledgeable, successful and approachable, how would you be dressed in their opinion? What suit, shirt, blouse, tie, skirt, shoes, watch, make-up and hairstyle would you be wearing? In their opinion – not yours."

?QUESTION #34: Do I have to buy the tapes you're lending me?

QUESTION FOR A QUESTION: Do you like the tapes you're listening to?

EASY ANSWER: I'd be willing to lend you the tapes so you can get started in developing your understanding of the business. At some point you will want your own library of tapes for your personal reference source.

FURTHER THOUGHT: This is not necessarily an objection. The prospect is looking for information upon which they can base an informed decision. Most people realize that the Quixtar registration fee won't be the only cost involved in running a business. This person wants to know what else can be expected. It's important to be honest. When I show the plan, I mention the registration fee plus a small investment in some introductory tools to get your business started.

You have already purchased the audios you have lent this prospect. They're part of what you call the tools of the trade. Your tools are the audios, books, and brochures that lead your prospect through the system. It's a training system. As part of our training system, audios, books and meetings are a recognized as a way to acquire knowledge, and skills, to improve performance in today's business world. Teachers, doctors, mechanics, and countless other professionals rely on training and motivation to learn industry trends, to stay focused, and to keep their skills up-to-date. Why shouldn't we?

Eventually, the prospect will want his own library of training materials and resources, but in the mean time, you will be happy to lend them to him so he can get started.

If you consistently allow people to borrow from you like a library, you are preventing them from thinking like a business owner. A real business owner owns his business and takes responsibility for it. It's necessary to empower people to take ownership which includes the decision to purchase and use the tools designed to build his business. As long as you lend audios, it's still your business.

Everything you tell them about the tools will be reinforced at live events. It won't take long for the new IBO to realize the importance of a commitment to the training system: reading, listening, and attending seminars.

?QUESTION #35: Do I have to buy 100 points of product every month?

QUESTION FOR A QUESTION: Do you want a bonus check every month?

EASY ANSWER: When you become an IBO you benefit from purchasing the products you use regularly. There is no minimum and/or maximum required each month. However, when you, your clients and members collectively buy 100 points, you validate the compensation plan and receive a bonus check.

FURTHER THOUGHT: The person asking this question may have a concern about being forced to purchase unneeded products. Assure her that our product line is focused on the products she uses on a daily basis.

There is no minimum purchase in a month. It's her business, and she can operate as she likes. She may purchase as much or as little as she wants.

We have over 500,000 products available through Quixtar and our partner stores. We focus on products that give us the best value for our money and that are replenishable. Of those, we know there are fifty items she is likely to use. That's why we show 100 points a month. We know she'll still have things she wants to buy commercially, even though Prosumerism is the key to her success.

We're looking to change her buying habits. She won't change what she buys, but the source she buys it from and the process she uses to buy it. When she becomes an IBO and is investing in her own future, she'll want to purchase the products that promote her own financial success.

The most important thing is that this is a volunteer business and you may choose what you feel comfortable purchasing.

?QUESTION #36: I've always shopped at Costco. How does this business compare?

QUESTION FOR A QUESTION: Does Costco offer its shoppers the opportunity to be an equity partner?

EASY ANSWER: It's tough to compare two companies in different industries. Costco profits on its shoppers. We profit by our shopping.

FURTHER THOUGHT: In business you're known by your competition. Coke vs. Pepsi; BMW vs. Mercedes; Home Depot vs. Lowe's; McDonalds vs. Wendy's. Many businesses fail because they don't understand who their competition is. Conversely, some businesses have thrived because they've realized who their competition really is.

Who do you consider to be our competition? If your answer is Wal-Mart, Costco or Target you're in trouble! These 'big box', deep discount stores compete on price only. Their goal is to sell TONS of stuff with tiny profit margins. Not all businesses compete on low prices. Convenience stores are a perfect example. Have you compared the price of a gallon of milk? How do convenience stores get away with it? Simple. Customers shop at convenience stores to save time, not money. They make it easy to shop. As a result, the time customers save is priced into each product. Convenience stores charge sky-high prices and still do lots of business because they understand that they're not in competition with the superstores on price.

We are in the business of building business builders. We are not in competition with any retail stores or web sites. Why? Because they can't offer shoppers what we can. There is something priced into the cost of our products that no one else has. We price 'opportunity' into our products.

Do Target, Costco, Wal-Mart, Circuit City offer opportunity in their products? There is no other store in the world that offers the same kind of thing at any price.

?QUESTION #37: I don't feel I could use 100 points of product every month.

QUESTION FOR A QUESTION: Would it help if I could show you what products you'd most benefit from to develop 100 points?

EASY ANSWER: Since our product line is focused on replenishing your household with products you use daily, I'm confident that a little knowledge about the products will help you change your buying habits.

FURTHER THOUGHT: Here we have an issue of product education. Even though the prospect may understand the concept of our business, she really hasn't grasped the potential of it yet. With over 50,000 products to choose from, there won't be an issue with her ability to accumulate 100 points of product in a month.

Initially, she may find it difficult to accumulate the full 100 points, and will need some support in determining which products are right for her. Encourage her to purchase the amount of product she feels comfortable with while you continue to educate her on our private label lines. Much like Costco® has the private label of 'Kirkland™' we offer several private label brands like Ocean Essentials®, Magna Bloc®, Artistry®, Nutrilite®, and Satinique®. These labels provide the best profitability to an IBO. These product lines are not 'plain wrap' or 'deep discount' cheap alternatives. Rather, they are high quality, high value products that outperform the competition. Survey after survey confirms it. People today want more natural, more innovative, simpler, longer-lasting products. They're interested in having what they need delivered to their door.

Eventually, her product knowledge will increase to the level where she not only uses more than 100 points worth of product, but she can also teach others how to do the same. This question can also be answered by reassuring her that she can develop an unlimited number of clients and members who also count toward her 100 points of product per month. Many business teams are duplicating a '300 point IBO' by stressing the inclusion of clients and members.

?QUESTION #38: The products seem expensive.

QUESTION FOR A QUESTION: What are you comparing them to?

EASY ANSWER: You'll find plenty of products on our web site that are very cost competitive. No store sells everything at the cheapest price. Let's start you off by finding a handful of products that would be the best value to you.

FURTHER THOUGHT: We can't expect the prospect to be familiar with our products. We can, however, help them with some research so they can compare apples to apples. We can also emphasize the key benefits to those products which include: superior quality, competitive cost, concentration, and the convenience of home delivery. Our products are environmentally friendly, thus satisfying the socially conscious.

You may save $5 going to the market down the street, but you had to get in the car, drive down to the store and get it. What's your time worth? It is important to compare apples to apples. You cannot compare an e-commerce catalogue business to Wal-Mart. That is not a fair comparison. The product may be less expensive at that store, but you cannot replace two things: your time and travel. No matter how much money you think you are saving at that store, you can't match the value of having someone to ship it to your door. You also avoid the intangibles of hauling your kids through the store, fighting traffic, and spending far more than you intended on impulse buying.

No one store sells everything at the cheapest price. Stores that specialize in one product line, such as electronics, can often give a better price than Quixtar. We can offer a convenient buying experience. You can get a high quality, guaranteed product delivered to your door, all with a profit paid back to you. Remember that the price of the product is secondary to the scope of the opportunity.

X. THE 21 CONVERSATION KEYS

It all boils down to this. You are the best person to make a decision about the right thing to say. This is your prospect. This is your business. This is your future.

I can't predict all the questions you'll hear. And I can't give you all the right answers. But I can give you 21 Conversation Keys that will guide you on your path to success. These Conversation Keys have been referenced throughout this book and are designed as conversation helpers. If you use them you will be known as a powerful and logical communicator.

Remember that our business doesn't protect you from life; it just leaves you armed for it. Your conversation skills with people determines the quality of your business life, your family life, and your social life. I hope you will use this book to enhance every area of your life. That is the ultimate victory.

1. THE BEST ANSWER IS THE EASY ANSWER.

A simple, honest, sincere response will show respect for the question and the person asking it.

2. BE YOURSELF.

Use words and phrases that feel comfortable for you. When you're comfortable with the response, others will sense your confidence.

3. HAVE FUN WITH THE PROCESS.

Lighten up! Keep a smile on your face, and laugh a little bit. Stay focused on your dreams and goals, but remember that success is a journey, not a destination. Resolve yourself to get results, have fun and win at this business. Joe Namath said, "When you win, nothing hurts."

4. DON'T TAKE IT PERSONALLY. TAKE IT PROFESSIONALLY.

Remember that people don't do things for you. People do things for themselves. The person asking the question is not questioning your truthfulness, sincerity or commitment. The person asking the question is trying to figure out whether this business venture is right for them. An emotional reaction to their question will confuse them at best. At worst, it will push them away.

5. MASTER YOUR EMOTIONAL REACTION TO QUESTIONS.

Emotional intelligence is the ability to manage and control your emotions. Be open to learning more about yourself, and understand why you respond that way so you can overcome the negative feelings that create in you a 'fight or flee' reaction. Practice those questions. Memorize and internalize the response that's most comfortable for you. Learn to control your emotional reaction.

6. BE PROFESSIONAL ALWAYS.

You are representing your whole organization. No matter how tempting, don't be drawn into defending yourself against someone who is negative. Politely and professionally extricate yourself from that situation. Keep your eye focused on your own future, and set an example of professionalism for your prospects and your team.

7. NEVER SLAM THE DOOR ON A PROSPECT.

The prospect may not be in the looking zone right now, but I've had many who have come back later and registered with someone else on our team. Circumstances change. The prospect remembers the last contact he had with this business, and that determines his opinion forever more. Let him leave with the thought that the business is a great opportunity, and that the individuals who proposed it to him were professional and had integrity.

8. NO PROSPECT IS THE ONLY OR LAST PROSPECT.

We're not looking for everybody. We're only looking for the "somebodys" who want to mark their own path to success. You can say all the right things, do all the right things, act in all the right ways and they still won't say 'yes'. Likewise, you can say all the wrong things, do all the wrong things, and act in all the wrong ways and they'll say 'yes'. The Law of Averages will serve you well. Keep talking to people.

9. USE THESE COMMUNICATION SKILLS IN ALL AREAS OF YOUR LIFE.

Remember, success is success is success. Treasure the skills you're developing in this business and transfer them to the other parts of your life – at work, at home, and with your friends and associates.

Your success in all of these areas will reflect your personal and professional development.

10. NOTHING REPLACES PRACTICE AND EXPERIENCE.

You'll become an expert with confident conversations based on the number of times you handle questions from new prospects. You can use this book as a reference/resource, but ultimately, experience is the best teacher. In addition to 'real life' experience, get together with other IBOs and role-play common questions and answers. My favorite quote on the subject is: "Tell me and I'll soon forget. Show me and I may remember. Let me try and I'll understand."

11. ANSWER A QUESTION WITH A QUESTION.

We have been conditioned to answer questions, not ask them. However, we can only learn by asking and listening. Program your mind to ask questions like; "Why do you say that?"; "Is there anything else?"; "What was your experience in the past?"

12. YOU DO NOTHING, YOU EARN NOTHING.

Everything in this business is earned. Sometimes people confuse 'activity' with production. Always remember this most powerful statement; "Nothing happens until you book a meeting!" End of discussion.

13. NOBODY WILL REQUIRE YOU TO DO ANYTHING.

Quixtar won't, your business support team won't, and I won't. If you wanted to make the income of an attorney, what would be required? Law School. The only thing that would require you to do anything in your business is the amount of income you want to make.

14. I KNOW HOW YOU FEEL, I FELT THE SAME WAY BUT WHAT I FOUND...

This phrase is one of the most relatable ways to respond to people's questions and objections.

15. SELL THE APPOINTMENT, NOT THE BUSINESS.

It is always best to get face-to-face with your prospects. I'd never recommend showing the plan over the phone or through email. On occasion however, you may have to. But when you do, remember you lose out on most of your non-verbal influence!

16. EVERYBODY HAS THE TIME TO DO THIS.

Remember that everyone has the same 24-hour day. People make time for the things that are important to them. Your communication skills and belief will influence their priorities. I've never met anyone who said they had the time to do this; however, I have met people who prioritized their time because this business is worth it.

17. THE FIVE P'S: PRIOR PLANNING PREVENTS POOR PERFORMANCE.

It's a simple 5-word sentence that successful people live by.

18. ASK FOR THE REGISTRATION.

Lead people into partnership with you and ask for the registration. "I think you'd be great and I'd enjoy working with you. I would like to register you in this business."

19. FIND YOUR PROSPECT'S PRIMARY MOTIVATING FACTOR.

More time, security, personal development, extra income, financial freedom, owning a business, personal or professional development, helping others, meeting new people, respect, recognition, retirement, or leaving a legacy, are all valid reasons for motivation.

20. WHAT YOU PROMOTE IS WHAT THEY INVESTIGATE.

If you promote an e-commerce, or home delivery service, your prospect will investigate it. If you promote their dream or the training system, your prospect will investigate that. Promote what you want your prospect to investigate.

21. BE SCHEDULED AND MOVING! BUSY PEOPLE GET THINGS DONE.

People want what they can't have. If a prospect feels like they are your only candidate, you lose your edge. However, if your prospect senses you are going to be developing some wealthy people and they have a shot at it, they'll be more responsive.

*   *   *

A FINAL WORD

You are engineered for success, designed for accomplishment and created with the seeds of greatness. Remember, if this business is good enough for you, it's good enough for anyone you will ever show it to. People would be lucky to associate with you and your team. Be proud of what you have and be confident! You can do it!